# Milk & Marrow

Breanna Leslie

Green Muse Studio

To my children, who saw me through the fog.

# Contents

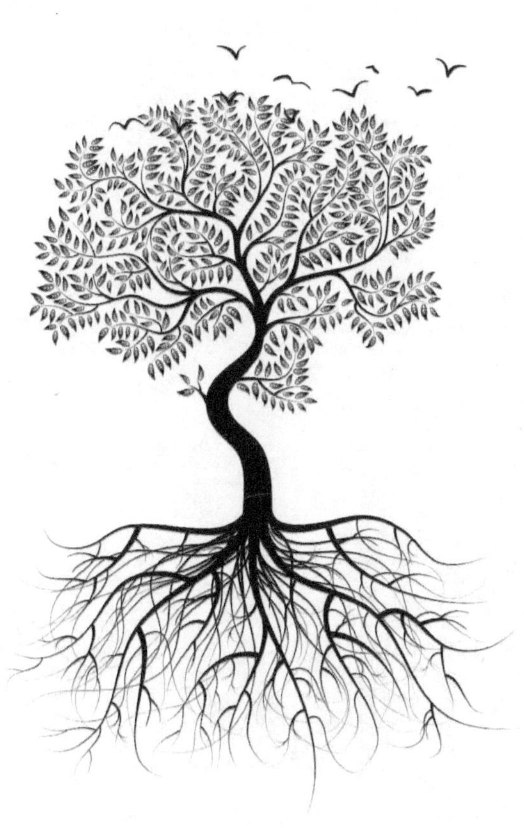

# Appalachia

I've never felt so at peace as I do
in the forest, leaves crunching beneath my feet,
shuffling past saplings straining for light
amongst the wiser trees.

Or when I push past the edge
and sink into the clearing,
where shadows stretch long and breezes gust
among the bees
that dance atop wildflowers,
bending to the whims of the wind.

I've never felt so rich as when I bask
in midday sun on a boat
that sways with the heartbeat

of a river most unruly,
curling around hayfields,
cutting through hills.

I've never felt so sleepy, so content,
as I do in the blue of a holler afternoon,
daylight still burning
on the other side of the mountain.

In these moments, I am whole—
bound to earth, yet drifting free,
a quiet soul among the leaves,
the river's pulse, the mountain's breath.
Here, I am as I was meant to be.

Appalachian.

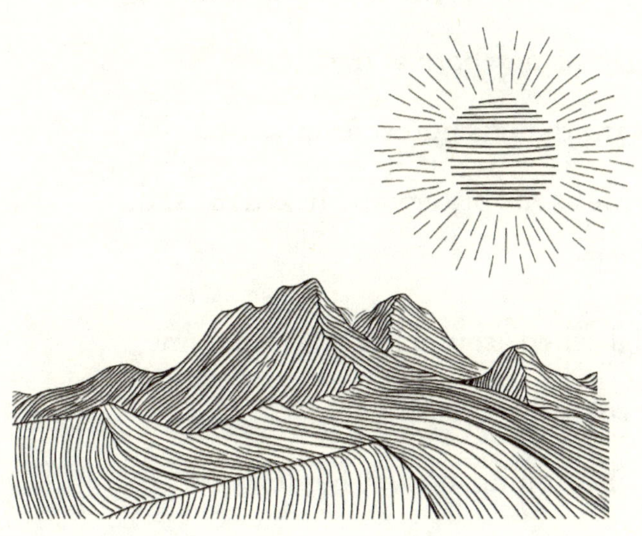

# Milk & Marrow

I came to the mountain, joints aching, head fogged,
a wriggling, pink newborn at my breast.
A baby—warmth in its purest form,
sustaining me as the bitter wind licked my skin.

My arms tightened around her bundled frame.
We drew a collective breath—
the journey beckoning, no way but forward,
and up.

The mountain, craggy and wild,
must have been conjured by God,
thrust from the earth like a geyser,
petrified in layered rock.
It loomed with the weight of permanence,

unmoved by our struggle,
its silence demanding reverence.

Muttered prayers and cries for help
echoed from the peak.
Further up but no less frightened and
exhausted from the trek.
I clung to their voices and the shaky promise of tomorrow—
knowing no promise is certain but the fate of stagnation is.

At times, the climb grew sharp,
rocks cutting into soles,
hunger gnawing at the edges of resolve.
I felt hollow—milk drained,
marrow scraped thin by the weight of the journey.

But she stirred at my chest,
a soft, rooting motion,
and I remembered:
we were forged of the same substance.

Milk and marrow.
Life's most fragile offerings,
yet enough to shape the world.

Still, it beckoned—
time waits for no one.
So we climbed, tangled in one another,
each step an act of faith.

# Harsh & Holy

I don't want the polished version of events,

The politician's collage of sunny hillsides and handshakes.

Our heritage doesn't exist at your convenience—

It doesn't brush the ugly under a braided kitchen rug.

These mountains hold their dirt-smudged intricacies like a basket,

Secure in their unkempt nature.

These woven vines, tucked in the trees,

Bear witness to the monstrosities dropped upon us

By mining companies and snake-oil salesmen,

Promising reprieve from pain and suffering.

Because the beauty of Appalachia exists within the dance

Of harsh and holy—

Where the bitter winds speak of struggle,

But the earth's hum whispers of healing,

And in the silence between, we find our breath.

Here, the blood of ancestors runs like rivers,

And the stars above know every sorrow and,

Every hope that rises from the ashes.

# Bloodline

I was born to feel my mother's pain,
And her mother's,
And her mother's,
And so on.

It's drawn to me like a magnet, and I welcome it,
A cosmic shock absorber, feeling every wrong completely
Until the pain runs out, so my children
And their children
Don't face the trickle-down economics of trauma.

They say cells have memory.
I can attest to this truth because my sadness isn't mine,
And my life hasn't been beer bottles and bruises.
Mostly, it was happy, filled with quiet moments of joy.

Yet, their depression hunts me down,
A cougar in the trees, waiting, watching,
Because it's found a home in me—a comfy place,
Worn down by years I haven't lived and boulders made smooth
As it takes the path of least resistance.

But it's time for me to put it away. I will be the end of this line,
The final port where the river of trauma stops flowing.
I won't be the funnel.
This river stops here, never to pollute my babies' streams
Or bleed into their oceans.□

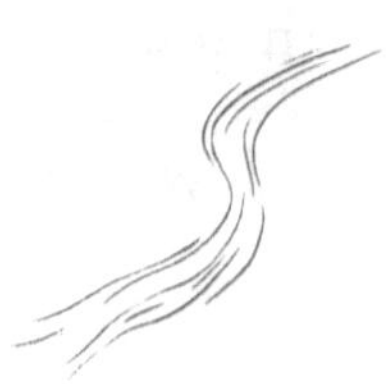

# Parasite

My second greatest fear is becoming my mother. It follows my greatest, which is passing this fear to my daughter. I worry I'll bruise her like a peach, that the bruise will spread, tainting the sweetness at her core. It terrifies me that she might cradle those bruises like a prized inheritance, tucking them beneath her mattress where they can fester unseen.

I fear that one day she'll look at herself and feel disgust—disdain blooming in her chest, a perfect mirror of the contempt she harbors for me.

One day, she'll swallow her emotions, quiet her screams, because she'll fear they're the sign she's been dreading: pieces of her mother surfacing unbidden. A symptom of rot, browning her once-bright flesh. Every twinge of anger will drag her into guilt. It's happening. I'm her. She's me.

And we're insane—wrapped inside this rot like a parasite, devouring the fruit from within.

# Rotten Fruit

I was raised by a broken woman with

Damage so deep the fruit of the next tree

Bruised bitter by the seed that let it grow,

A peach, so ripe but unappealing,

I roll myself in sugar

To tame my flavors

# Cracked

If you cracked me open,

I reckon my blood would pour out

Like a mountain spring on the

First sunny day of march.

It might search for earth's

Dimples to rest from its journey.

My bones might reach to the sky

Like mountaintop cedars

The air might whistle from my lungs

Breeze through branches

And my soul might roll like a mid-summer

Gully-washer, spitting mud and shale

At the feet of mother Appalachia

# We Fought Today

We fought today.

My fist plunged into the glass of your delusion,
and your edges sliced my flesh,
sour drops of reality glistening on the floor.
My fingers dab at the sticky,
globules resistant to the light.

You wince, turn away—
a scene too threatening to absorb,
the truth of time and tortured tradition.
Eyes wide, I drink it in, lapping it up,
tongue on soil like a ravenous dog.

Belly full, bloodline tangled,

I nap in the blinding light of truth.

# Mending

We’re never really whole, just as
We’re never really separate.

Did you know trees speak to one another?
Echoes of their mothers tremor in the soil.
Voices ferrying curses and well-spent grace,
Onward through time and craggy rock.

Entangled—we go forth.
Trees, milkweed, daughters,
Wearing thorns we didn’t ask for,
And blight we didn’t earn.

Yet, branches shoot skyward,
And still, seeds fall—

Certain the earth will catch them.

Trusted as the sun rising,

Murmurs pulse in earthen grounds.

In winding rootways,

Ancestors press their palms against the dark—

A quiet mending beneath our feet.

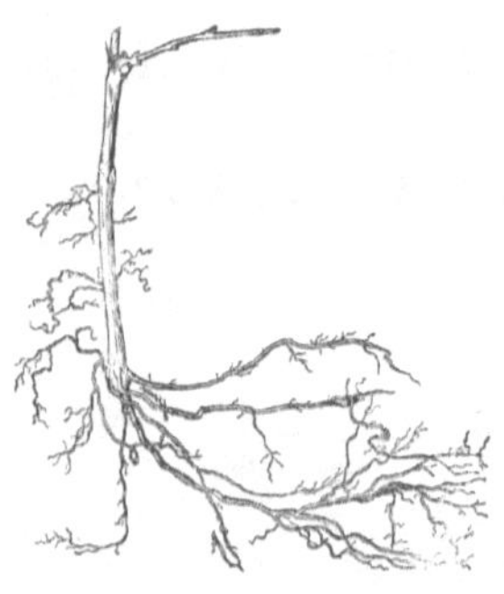

# Mimosa Tree

A mimosa tree hangs low and sleepy
Over a grave tipped sideways from
Time and buckling ground

Fireflies flicker at the edge,
Emerging from a golden sea of hay.

And I rest my back comfortable against
The bark, that bites through cotton.

Night song warms their melodies
Frogs and crickets a backdrop
For God's paint strokes.

I relish the quiet cacophony

Here but not here

Barely a whisper but big enough

To fill the July air

Warm and sweet, pink petals raining down.

And here I sit in time's irrelevance

Amongst roots and graves

Bones and blooms

Above and below

I rest in the middle,

Caught between

Memories and questions of what awaits.

There is peace in nature's noise

And comfort in her thorns.

And so I sit,

At home in the graveyard

Beneath the mimosa

Where bodies and souls

Return to their maker

And I--

Their willing audience.

# Bejeweled in Pink Flowers

To grow up Appalachian
is to revere and curse the mountains
in one hungry breath—
to hate the poverty-stricken stalemate
between roots and wings.

To be Appalachian
is to sink bare toes into cool summer grass,
to call your mamaw for supper,
to cut class for the first day of deer season.

To know things hide beneath the shadows
of mountains—human and inhumane—
but that joy still calls
from their misty crowns,

bejeweled in pink flowers.

To stay Appalachian,
one must simply live.
For our mothers' spring-fed blood
fills our stills.

# I Prefer the Trees

I prefer trees to people.
Sharp, jutting arms reaching toward heaven,
The more gnarled, the better.

Bend my eye with a grotesque figure--
And solidify my smallness
Beneath a shaking canopy of green.

Rake my gaze up and down
Jagged bark, its prints
dripping with moss,
And remind me of nature's tattered splendor.

# Sunburnt & Sane

I see my dad everywhere,

But mostly in pine trees,

Specifically—

The ones pierced by

Lemonade sunsets in midsummer,

The ones that paint asphalt

In ripples like the wake

On the Ohio River.

And then I'm in the boat,

Five again,

Eating Doritos and drinking RC cola,

Arranging rubber worms

By color in tackle boxes,
Sandpaper carpet prickling my thigh,
One-piece swimsuit dragging
Across lobster-red skin.

Life is good here
As he casts another line,
His hands brown, wrapped around the reel.

He gets a bite,
Sets the hook with a smile,
And then it's over—
A memory washed away with the current.

It's all just dappled sunlight on patchy roads,
And I'm thirty-three,
Longing to be sunburnt and sane.

*Previously published in Basilisk Tree

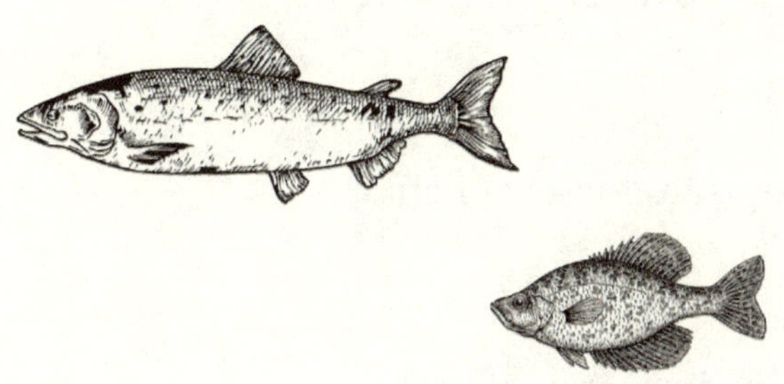

# Linear

Aquamarine sky over choppy water

I lie on my back

On red carpet, that stinks of fish

Dad casts a line in search of bass

And mom lights a cigarette

Life is good here under the midday sun

And I know my bed will sway with phantom waves tonight

I know this moment will cling to the fibers of the universe

At least,

For a little while

And if time is neither here nor there,

Then and now—

If it is as the theorists say, that nothing is linear,

Maybe I can pull that magic through and,

Siphon it back into my life

Maybe–

I can pour it onto their heads like

Holy water

*Previously published in Gypsophila Magazine

# Funeral

How foolish we are
to fight over the dead
like scavengers of war,
picking through the remnants
of diamonds and dust,
hoarding lives
in closets for safe-keeping.

How selfish to ignore
the empty husk left behind,
filling hungry pockets
while the body is cold.

But you—
you died without pennies, dimes, or fanfare.

You died and left nothing but
stifling air in a muggy September house,
your stained camo ball cap slouched on the recliner,
your shoes still by the door.

No luxury of wills or savings bonds,
only my grief and childhood,
crushed under the weight of your casket
as they lowered you into the grave.

How selfish we are,
to use death as a springboard

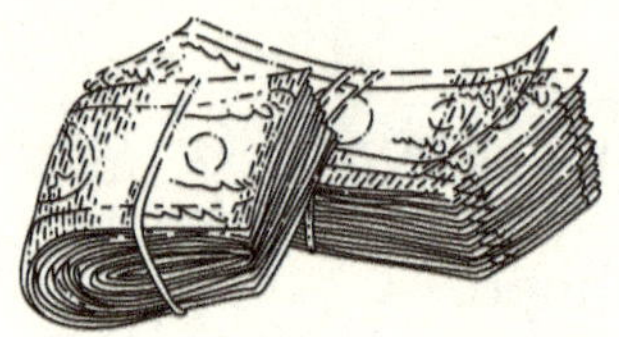

# Digging to China

Sometimes I miss you so desperately,

My chest becomes a cavern—

Earth splitting trenches of longing

That crack bone and time in

Simultaneous violence, unclaimed

By even the devil.

Gulleys so deep, I can swim through hell

And kiss angels on the other side.

Digging holes to China...

They said.

I'd dig,

And dig,

And dig,

Til I could see the streetlights of China

If it meant I'd see you again.

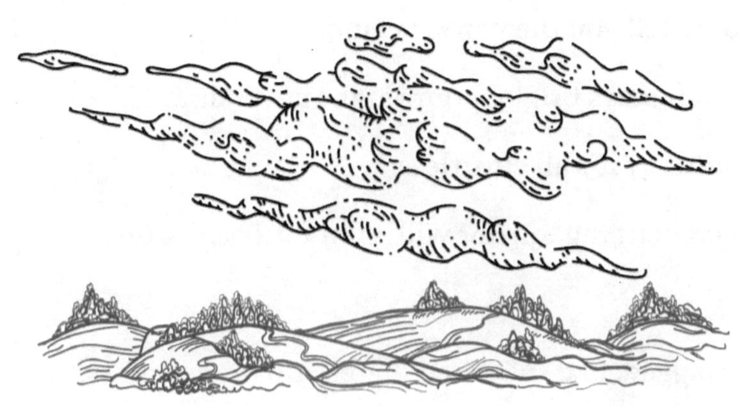

# Letter to my Inner Child

I wish I could tell you the world is kind,

That your hair stays bright, your thighs never dimple.

I wish I could say it's all effortless,

Molten glass bending to your will, your loftiest dreams.

But you're jagged, like shattered plates and broken glass.

A mosaic of pain, anger, and fear.

Dear girl, you aren't smooth like fairy tales or pink satin.

You aren't champagne in a crystal flute, but that doesn't mean you don't shine.

The last rays of an August sunset hit your edges,

Casting kaleidoscopes of colors on your heavy heart.

Jagged as you are, you are the sum of your parts.

Broken, smashed, cracked by hot and cold, anger, fear, and despair.

Jagged but not without color.

You don't fit perfectly into a mirror's frame.

You don't perform like a sleek art nouveau sculpture.

No, you take your jaggedness, your sharpest shards, and your colors.

And you lay them out to mend,

With shiny lead melted down from unfulfilled dreams.

And you create.

Sweet girl, you don't know it yet, but you were put here to create.

With all those shades and jagged pieces you've been dealt.

You birth mosaics that catch all the splendid rays of dawn, dusk, and the fullest moon.

You are stained glass, born from the need

To bathe a room in vibrant hues, to shine like a beacon for desperate hearts.

You tell stories to be passed down,

To your children, their children, and their children's children.

You are the keeper of memories and a warning to trespassers.

Do not bother.

Shatter her, and she will rebuild.

She will change her mosaics and continue to cast her colors,

Because she is stained glass, unbreakable and radiant.

# Recasting the Mind

Splay my brain open
Slice it down the middle like
Seventh grade biology

So we might sand
Down the prickly bits
And dull the jaggedness
Smooth it down to nothing

To the beginning
Before thoughts became coarse,
And lobes shattered into
Disjointed shards
Incapable of cooperation
Grind it to dust

So we might recast the clay
With long-wept tears
Throw it a thousand times
Until the grit is gone
And glaze grips the surface
Smooth like placid water

Painless

Mold it until it's
Something new
Something that shines like porcelain
And doesn't bite when you touch it

# Locked Out

I am one generation removed from the trauma in my tree,
But I'm still waiting outside,
Of the door my mother locked,
So many years ago—
Still locked outside the moment
When it happened.

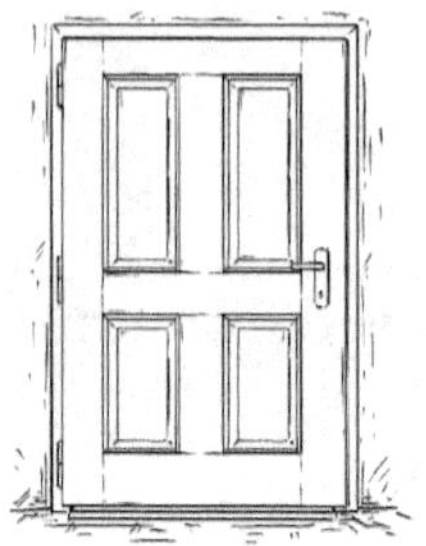

# Drowning

Motherhood drowned me

Four times over.

And with each gasping breath,

I tasted a new flavor of myself

# Russian Doll

Two fingers looped through
the handle of a three-day-old
mug of Folgers, a tomb of aging creamer,
a dead fly floating on its back.

My feet, bare and tired, shuffle
past the refrigerator to stare—
mindlessly—through the hazy window,
overlooking a melting landscape.

It's been twelve days since
the first sniffle rang out
like a gunshot of condemnation,
and a virus ravaged our home—
flames under gasoline,

throats blistered like acid.

I drop the mug into lifeless water.
My palms rest heavy on the counter,
framed by days of dirty dishes.

And for a moment,
I crack the lid on my walking coffin.
Like a nesting doll emerging from its mother,
I peek at my enclosure,
where instinct made a nest
as I withdrew.

Bleak as yellow wallpaper,
I lower the lid.
Dissociation calls.

# *The Fog*

The fog
dragged me past
the devil's flirtation—

inadvertent savior,
she drowned my body's
feverish pleas
to retreat back to Hades.

To dip my fingers into Styx,
ring the bell.

Savior she may be,
she's numb
to my praise—

a steward of the universe,

she cares not about my fate.

Shackled to time,

and blissfully unaware,

she settles with us,

in the trenches.

# Vaccination

Bearing children
was a noxious vaccination—
against pockets of resentment,
hiding just beneath the surface.

Motherhood coaxed it out.
Smoke to bees,
fox to hound.

She douses the unseen parts
in sunlight,
letting eager leaves unfurl,
rot slipping from bone.

# Bottled Decay

I wish I could bottle the decay of autumn,
wear it like a perfume—
maybe bathe in it,
on days when life buzzes with anticipation, agitation.

With smoke and petrichor clinging to my hair,
I might douse the screaming pleas to busy myself.

Bury my nose in the fibers of my sweater,
inhale the earth as it falls asleep.

Let my limbs still as the wind quiets,
a bed of leaves to cradle my bones,
a blanket of decay to quiet my thoughts.

# Mother Spaces

I've been dipping my toes into disappearing,

but the water's a little cold—

taste-testing loneliness, but the liquor burns bold.

Easing my way into isolation,

but my demons won't sell.

Smother me in noise, wrap me in thorns,

drown me in unrelenting duty.

I know my place—

toe the line of miracles and mania,

where mothers go to grieve

the girls they were, the women they'll never be.

This is where we go

when hot showers turn into tears,

when parking lots double as confessionals,

and mirrors only reflect ruins.

# Mother Masked

Sometimes, I search for my smile in the mirror—
not the mask I wear for functions
or weekly grocery runs,
but the genuine grin I once wore
after laughing until my ribs ached.
I practice.
My face contorts, strains in vain,
seeking the soft curve
that once nestled into thirty years
of laugh lines.

Lately, the crinkles and wrinkles
settle too easily into an exhausted frown
despite my prodding.
It's right there, like a word on the tip of my tongue,

yet it evades me,
leaving the face in the mirror
strangely disconnected, foreign.

It seems my joy is quieter these days,
but that's okay—
even the most breathtaking sunsets
are often veiled by clouds.

# If I lie here long enough

If I lie here long enough,
in this bed of lichen,
might the earth seep
back into me—

might roots take hold
of my broken pieces,
thread through ribs,
mending them—
one green bud at a time?

Might the ancient stones
cradle my tired frame,
like a babe in her mother's arms,
safe in the hollow of her curves?

Might the evening breeze

nuzzle my skin,

soft as a lover's goodbye?

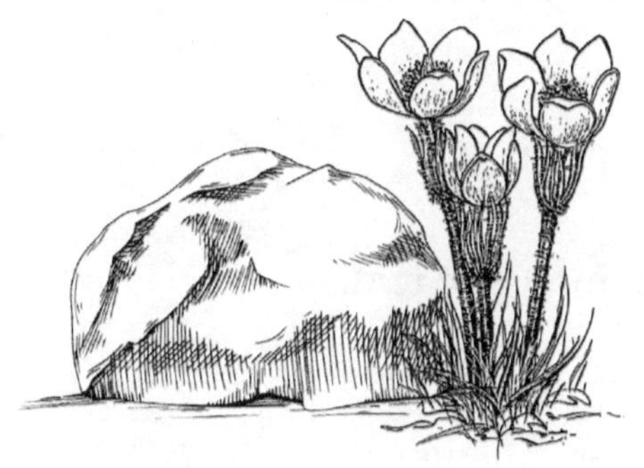

# Evolution

I used to miss my blonde hair—
the baby-white locks curling thick down my back.
In the mirror, I'd see
frizzy waves resting on my shoulders,
dark like mud, tired.

I'd grimace at the plainness of it all—
dull.
No longer Barbie-perfect,
a trophy made for admiring.

My mother once turned up her nose
at its deepening hue.
With the fading of my blondeness went
strangers' compliments, my confidence, her fondness.

But now, my daughter watches me
watch myself in the mirror.

Her expression, warm as the sun,
softens the sharpness of my gaze.

I see brown, not like mud, but earth—
rich, alive.

Like an Americano in a clear glass mug,
amber swirls hugging the edges.
and like butterscotch candies passed
from my father's hand to my once-pudgy palm.

I used to miss my blonde hair,
but now I see the comfort
in its quiet evolution.

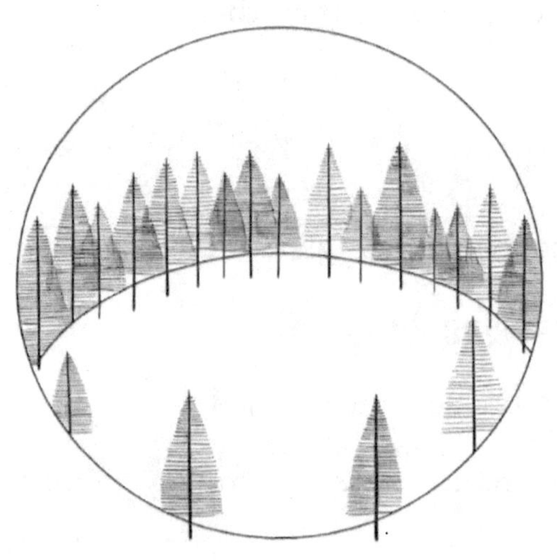

# Life Erupts

The air is changing
Brisk gusts dipped in petrichor
And foggy blankets
soothing an eager landscape

Spring is on the horizon
And I can taste its unfurling

Sun beams awaken
Sleepy forest spirits and
Bird song soothes
Winter's inertia into submission

Life erupts in response
Hatching verdant chaos under eager buds

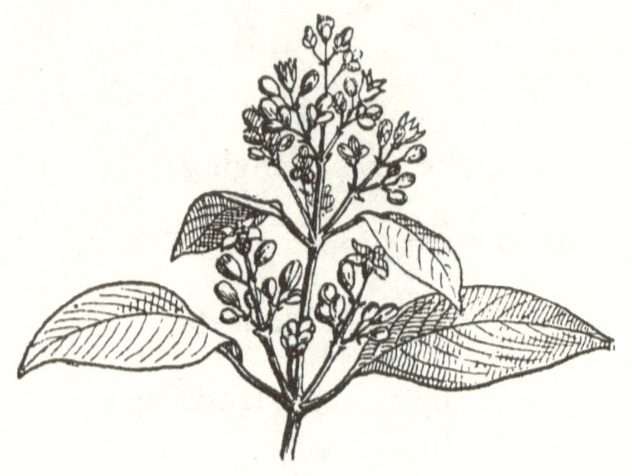

# Unremarkable

Aspiring to be
unremarkable.
I have children—
one, two, three, four—
wiping behinds, cleaning hands,
slaughtering lunches
of prepackaged meat.

Not noteworthy,
I carry on,
kissing boo-boos, making beds,
surgically cleaning
our modest homestead.

Unremarkable as leaves

offering pinpricks
of warm orange light on our faces
as we tromp past
a pad of soft green moss.

Ordinary as the crow
swooping over the lush hayfield
primed for cutting,
or the cow laboring
among the herd,
welcoming new life
without pomp or circumstance.

I strive not for glory,
but to lie in contentment,
in shadow.

# Magic of Smallness

I think my dad wanted me to leave.
He's long gone now, but his words
rattle around in my head like loose screws.

Accomplish something.
Go to school.
Think big.

And I did leave the mountains,
half a score ago, to the coast
where Spanish moss hangs lazily,
like sleepy fairies.

And though the sights
and balmy nights took

my breath away,
I was a stranger to blue water.

The mountains beckoned,
and the urge to bury myself
between two peaks festered.

It makes sense, being
a daughter of the hills,
but I suspect something more.

Perhaps there's spirit in the soil,
magic in the air,
an essence in the water,
sirens in the streams.

Maybe you spend enough time here—
bare feet on the land,
fingers plucking honeysuckle
from nested vines—

and Appalachia seeps in.
It swirls in your blood,
changing DNA,
marking every cell:
"This one's mine."

And so I went—
home, to let my body
commune with the mystics.

Because I don't think big.
I think about the roots of forest ferns
and bees resting on petals.

I bask in the magic of smallness.

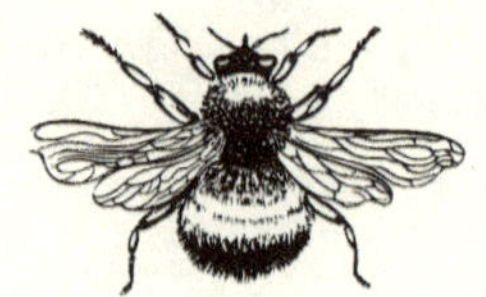

# Respiration

There is no respiration without you.
Poison gathers in my
medulla oblongata like resin,
hardening my thoughts,
pinning them down
like the wings of a moth
against canvas.
I look on—
praying for hands to break the glass,
for a gentle breeze to withdraw my death.

I need you like the last breath of oxygen
on a dying planet.
I need you to untangle the nest of torment
woven deep in muscle,

snared in spurred bone and jagged history.

Without you, my petals wither,

my stem collapses—

and I succumb to the inevitable.

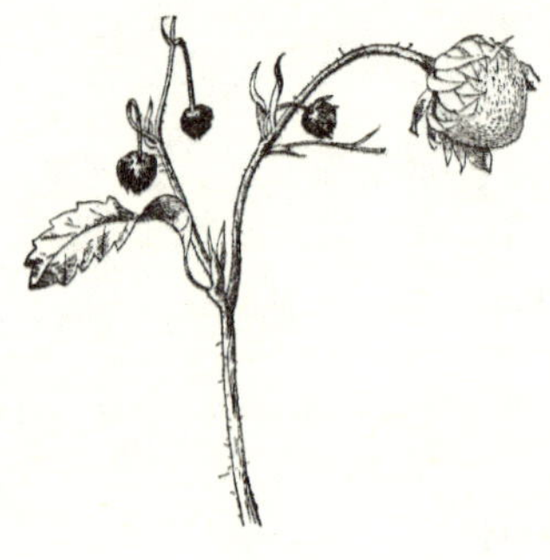

# Centurion

Tell me your secrets and I'll guard them with my life,
whisper your insecurities and I'll bury them like the dead.
Mother you, forever, I will.

I am your keeper—on the frontline when the battle comes,
or in the shadows, where your independence takes root.
Sacred duty runs through wombs and branches
far above my perch on the family tree.

I will mother you and your brothers, your passengers
as life carries you down the stream. Limbs
ready to snatch you from the rapids if you fall,
hammers steady, prepared to rebuild your boat.

This station is mine, anchored in blood and bone,

and I accept the role, steeled in it
like a centurion, forever on guard,
watching over the path you travel.

# Gilded Tapestry

My soul first met theirs in a dream, a vivid tableau of faceless bundles wrapped in flannel, facing a future I couldn't comprehend. Yet, I knew them. We had reached through the universe to find each other, weaving threads that formed a breathtaking landscape of rolling hills and deep valleys. Yellow sun rays bled into shadows as wild flora encroached on our path, sometimes marred with dangers seen and unseen.

I often trace the paths we've carved, reliving each trial as if it were the present. I retrace steps, rehearsing alternatives, knowing the road will repeat itself. I gaze back, the golden threads dull and frayed, abused by reflection, yet still calling for more.

Emerald meadows faded to muddy brown, and blue skies fell gray. Still, I take in the sights with gleaming fondness, even as the sands of time betray me. Nothing is as crisp as the first time you meet it, nor as vivid as the now. Eyes cast back fail to enjoy the wondrous journey ahead or notice the edge of silk slipping through trembling fingers.

# *Six*

There's a family of evergreens behind my house,
six in a row, their weathered trunks
nestled deep in the brush.
I stare at them often from my kitchen window,
and sometimes, I like to think,
they stare back—
six in a row,
rooted in permanence,
peering into my soul.

They stand untroubled by time,
witnesses to what came before
and what will come after—
after me, after us,
all six of us,

bound together

by roots we cannot see

and a legacy we cannot hold.

But sometimes, my hands plunged in soapy water,

the edges of time soften.

Roots and bones coalesce,

the present dissolving into what's to come,

and I have to wonder—

am I staring at the beginning?

or at the end?

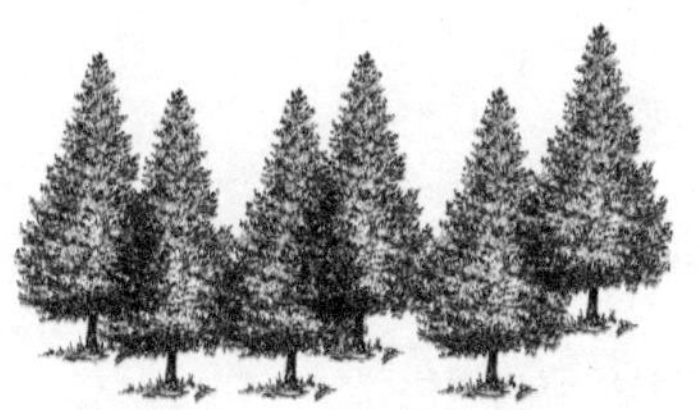

# Joy

Joy eluded me for some time.

She darted past, slunk into corners—

prey animal of the brain.

Timid as a hare,

rare as a mink,

she hid herself diligently,

for years.

Until one day,

in the wee hours of dusk,

I hovered over the steaming coffee.

From my periphery,

the elusive shadow of joy

scrambled through the kitchen—

tripping over Hot Wheels and Barbies,
clinging to the walls
like a feral cat forced inside.

Determination swelled—
bolstered by caffeine
and false confidence.

False fortune or not,
I strode behind her,
unbothered by her nervous howl.

She ricocheted from wall to wall,
desperate to maintain the distance between us,

only to find she'd met the end.
No more dark corners,
no recessed cavities of my mind.

Nowhere to hide.

And so,
Joy did the only thing she could.

She sank her haunches into the mirror.
Reflection swallowed her whole,
gobbling her up like hungry water.

Until she was safe in the glass—
tucked away,
trapped.

I stared into her eyes—
happy, but bloodshot—
and I dare not describe the feeling.

For it didn't fit like a glove or sweater—
more like the sticky cling of latex,

the kind that makes your skin sweat and itch.

Finally, tired of seeking answers,

I said simply,

“Speak violence to me, so I might understand your tone.”

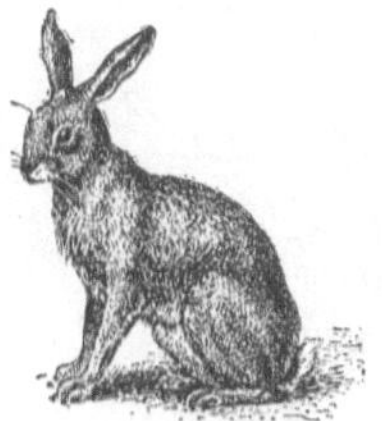

# Hugging the Line

While driving, my mind wanders to the shoulder

Where the road surrenders to the chaos of flesh and asphalt.

A sleepy driver, unexpected deer.

My mind calculates the risk

And how often it's brushed

Past my leg like a cat,

Teased death like fish on a bobber.

And I have to wonder how many near misses or hits

Have steered my life back across the white line.

How close have I come to an ending most somber?

# Rich Indulgences

What if our soul's only purpose
in life was to touch—
to wade through the physical
in an ocean of spirit?

What if our earthly goal
was to feel the weight
of a baby on your chest,
a toddler on your lap—
to hold the heaviness
of their absence once they've grown?

What if we were put here
to savor the smooth, creamy sweetness
of cheesecake,

the bubbles on your tongue—
Moscato on your tenth anniversary
at the edge of an ocean,
salt lingering on your skin?

What if you were put here
to weather the subtle burn
of leering eyes on your neck,
a vexed lover pacing
the bleachers of a high school football game—

or the hungry bristle of a spring breeze
against goose bumped skin,
the sharp breath of March thirty-first,
its promise of warmth still distant?

What if human existence means
Savoring the sinking weight
In the pit of your stomach
As you watch your parents

Lowered six feet into the earth?

Maybe these bodies are nothing
But a collection of cells wired to feel
The fibers of the universe
Knitted and knotted into
Peaks and valleys of a life?

What if the entire act of living was a rich indulgence?

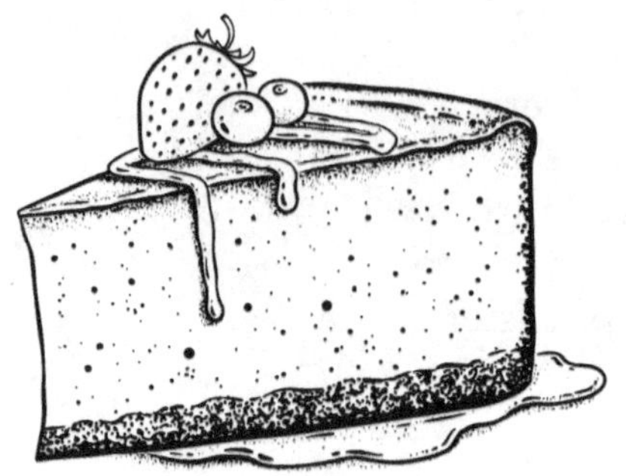

# Let Them

Tease out the static, let your brain breathe. Feel the steam of fresh coffee settle on your lip.

The day's not that bad—she will emerge, fanfare or not, just as she always does.

Sometimes, there's relief in letting:

Let the world unfold. Let people be. Let yourself follow instinct.

Life was never meant to stretch to splinters,

but to flow, softly.

# Casting Shadows

Daffodils dance by a roadside sign,
bending in our wake as we speed past,
post-tee ball ice creams melting in hand.

The iridescent sky bleeds scarlet
where it kisses the earth, and I can feel it—
the moment, whole and golden,
gritty as sweat on skin.

But sweet contentment is fleeting,
as legs grow gangly and baby teeth fall.
The golden hour of childhood glimmers like magic,
And though time casts shadows,
The light lingers still

# Surrealism

How surreal it is to be thirty-three,
Standing in my eight-year-old daughter's
Bedroom, amid messy pink sheets,
A soft lamp, and a hungry wind
Whistling at the window,
Where finches nest,
Overlooking a powdery dusting of snow
On a frigid January day—

Three boys downstairs, digesting
Lunch and '90s cartoons,
Painted orange in nostalgia,
In a pocket of time
Where I used to play.

How surreal it is to sink

My fingers into their warm laundry—

Faded T-shirts and stained socks—

And wash their dishes,

Where cornbread mixed with Nutella,

And laughter with tears.

Four bounding children, growing, clashing—

Waves against unyielding rocks.

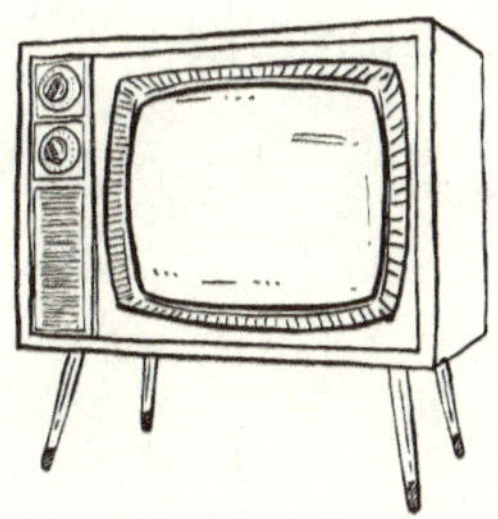

# Prose

My only hope for growing older
Is that I age like prose—
Sprinkled, no—
Etched on a page, creeping further
Past the coffee ring
And the questionable stain
On the left margin.

I hope my presence gains meaning
As I march past the lines—
Gaining thunder,
Gaining wonder,
Each mark a story,
Each smudge a truth.

The end of the page

Races to meet me like a wave,

Or a cliff—

Both stains and fine blue lines

Are irrelevant now,

Lost in the weight of words.

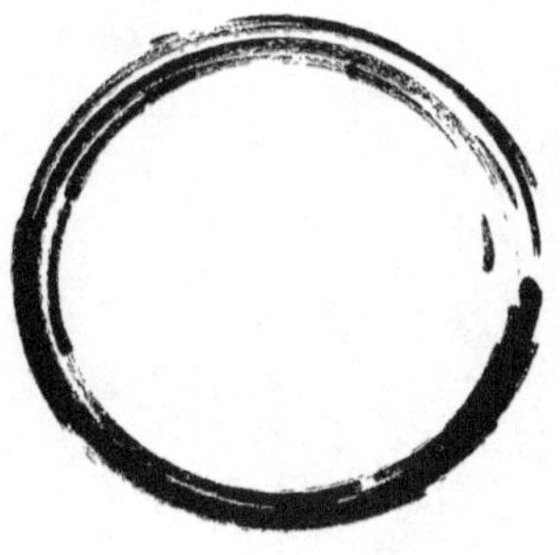

# I do not ask for much

I do not ask much of this life or the world

Only that my absence from it

Is felt

By somewhere,

By someone

Lovingly.

# Worlds Collide

If I go before you,
Just know I'll write my love
On the threads of spider webs,
Collecting dew like stars
To shimmer in the morning sun.

If I'm gone, please know
I'll whisper to you from the edge
Of every snowflake that
Lands in your hair.

And if you're still here,
Missing me and my mess,
Know you'll find me
In the tall summer grass,

Dancing in the wind as
Orange rays fall behind
That old, rusty barn roof.

You'll find me in every
Flower that blooms,
Bee that buzzes,
Puddles splashing beneath the children's rain boots.

Find me in the steam
Twirling above a mug of hot chocolate,
The ring left behind
From Jack's chocolate milk,
The pile of paintbrushes on Millie's dresser,
Hayes' wild moves and love of story,
And in the way Colter squeezes your neck.

Look for me in everything,
Until our worlds collide once more.

www.ingramcontent.com/pod-product-compliance
Lightning Source LLC
LaVergne TN
LVHW090532110826
845146LV00003B/1072

* 9 7 9 8 9 8 7 9 1 0 2 1 4 *